Writing for Business

Pocket Mentor Series

The *Pocket Mentor* Series offers immediate solutions to common challenges managers face on the job every day. Each book in the series is packed with handy tools, self-tests, and real-life examples to help you identify your strengths and weaknesses and hone critical skills. Whether you're at your desk, in a meeting, or on the road, these portable guides enable you to tackle the daily demands of your work with greater speed, savvy, and effectiveness.

Books in the series:

Leading Teams
Running Meetings
Managing Time
Managing Projects
Coaching People
Giving Feedback
Leading People
Negotiating Outcomes
Writing for Business
Giving Presentations

Writing for Business

Expert Solutions to Everyday Challenges

Harvard Business School Press

Boston, Massachusetts

Printed in the United States of America

11 10 09 08 07 5 4 3 2 1

Library of Congress Cataloging-in-Publication Data

Writing for business : expert solutions to everyday challenges.

p. cm. — (Pocket mentor series)

Includes bibliographical references.

ISBN 978-1-4221-1472-8 (pbk. : alk. paper)

1. Business writing. I. Harvard Business School Publishing Corporation.

HF5718.3.W745 2007

808'.06665—dc22

2007000877

The paper used in this publication meets the requirements of the American National Standard for Permanence of Paper for Publications and Documents in Libraries and Archives Z39.48-1992

Contents

Mentor's Message: Reader-Focused Writing Gets Results

To be successful, businesspeople need to use the latest and best strategies. This Pocket Mentor will update you on effective processes for writing everything from a simple memo to a proposal. You'll see how putting readers' needs first can help clarify (streamline) your writing and extend your influence as a manager. This book contains easy-to-follow steps on how to

- Organize your documents to target your readers' needs
- Jump-start your writing assignments to overcome procrastination
- Apply editing and design principles to drive action and decisions

When you apply these proven strategies, you'll see the results in your writing productivity and document quality. In fact, your readers will comment on the difference!

Best of luck!

Deborah Dumaine, Mentor

Deborah Dumaine is the president and founder of Better Communications, a learning company that delivers globally recognized business, leadership, technical, financial, and sales writing workshops. Since 1978, nearly 100,000 learners have attended Better Communications' workshops. Ms. Dumaine is the author of *Write to the Top: Writing for Corporate Success* (Random House) and the *Instant-Answer Guide to Business Writing* (iUniverse). She also has contributed sections on business writing to the *World Book Encyclopedia.* Ms. Dumaine holds BA and MA degrees from Smith College. For further information, please see her Web site at www.writetothetop.com.

Writing for Business: The Basics

Foundation Principles

The difficulty is not to affect your reader, but to affect him precisely as you wish.

—Robert Louis Stevenson

EFFECTIVE BUSINESS WRITING rests on a few foundation principles. If you master them, you'll know how to handle the many different writing tasks that come your way.

Clarify your purpose

When you set out to write a business document, the first thing you should ask yourself is, "Why am I writing this document?" Business writing serves many purposes.

- **Explain or justify actions:** "Because all of the bids we received from our current vendors were high, we decided to reject them and seek others."
- **Convey information:** "Management wants all employees to know that quarterly sales of our new product exceeded expectations."
- **Influence readers:** "The engineering team can meet these deadlines."

- **Deliver good or bad news:** "Unfortunately, the engine fire you reported occurred one day after the expiration of the warranty."

- **Request action:** "The design team should complete and deliver all product specifications by May 1."

Keep your purpose in mind as you begin writing. Many writers, in attending to the mundane tasks of preparing a document, lose track of their purpose. Here's one way to avoid that problem: jot down your purpose at the beginning of your draft, and refer to it as you proceed. When you've finished your draft, review it to make sure it fulfills your initial purpose.

Take a reader-centered approach

Just as a company won't connect with its customers if it fails to consider their needs and attitudes, you won't connect with *readers* if you don't understand them, their desires, and the way they prefer to receive information.

Thinking, drafting, organizing, and editing from your reader's point of view improves clarity and drives action. If readers understand what you are trying to convey and what their next steps should be, their jobs will be much easier.

Why is a reader-centered approach important? Consider the true story of a company that failed to analyze its audience when writing what seemed to be a simple postcard announcing a change of address. Neglecting to put itself in its readers' shoes, the company forgot to include one of the most vital pieces of information: the date

What Would YOU Do?

Attention Span

ROGER HAS TO SEND a memo to the field sales staff explaining the department's planned rollout of its spring catalog, which will describe all new and existing products. He wants to alert the staff to the time of the catalog's completion and delivery, and he wants to remind them to submit the names and mailing addresses of all the customers who should receive it. He's in a quandary about how to structure his memo.

He could begin with a paragraph on the purpose of the catalog and then describe some of its high points or features. Eventually, he'd want to remind his readers about sending in all customer addresses by February 15. "It will probably take me half a page or so to say all of this," he thinks. "I wonder how much of it they'll actually read?" What would you do if you were in Roger's shoes?

of the move. Customers knew *where* to reach the company, but not *when* they should use the new address.

State your key message clearly

Once you identify the purpose of your document and have considered your audience, isolate the key message you want your readers to remember. This message should be clear and concise—usually stated in only one or two sentences. For example, "To meet our customer's delivery deadline, we must complete the product design by May 1."

In many cases, your key message will be stated at or near the very beginning of the document; the rest of the document will be used to flesh out the details and to answer the question "Why?" or "What are the implications of what I am proposing?"

For greatest clarity, stick to one topic per document. If you find that you have two unrelated key messages, write two documents.

Keep the message short and simple

Busy readers appreciate concise documents. In fact, shorter is better as long as the document communicates the required information. Keeping your document short ensures that your key message stands out. Economy of words also saves your readers valuable time. Consider the following example:

> *At her boss's suggestion, and with the help of corporate counsel, Joan wrote an apologetic letter to the five disgruntled customers who threatened to sue.*

As a writer, your challenge is to know when a sentence has reached its optimal carrying capacity. In the preceding example, knowledge of the audience is a useful guide. Do the readers need to know that Joan's boss suggested the letter or that corporate counsel was brought in? Is it relevant that there were *five* disgruntled customers or that they threatened to sue? If these bits of information are not necessary, consider cutting them.

Your sentence would then read as follows:

Joan wrote an apologetic letter to the disgruntled customers.

NOTE: Whether they are reading, looking, or listening, your audience may not give you their full attention. So don't overload them with nuances and details that compete with your main message for their attention. The main message must stand out.

Confirm your delivery strategy

Even a well-written document will lose its impact if it doesn't come from the right person, at the right time, and in the right format. So before you begin writing, consider who should originate the communication. Should it come from you? Your boss? The entire team? The choice is bound to make a difference in reader impact.

Also consider whether you are writing your document too early or too late. If you write too early, people won't be ready to focus on the issue you're raising. If you wait too long, you'll lose the opportunity to make a suggestion or prevent a problem.

Finally, the format of your writing will also affect its impact. When you choose a format, consider your purpose, your audience, and the information you want to convey. For example, to dissemi-

Steps for Planning Your Writing Task

- Clarify your purpose for writing.
- Analyze your audience.
- Isolate and refine your bottom line.
- Plan your writing strategy.

nate the findings of a customer satisfaction survey, you could send an e-mail summary of the report to the entire company and provide details on how to obtain the entire report. You might also invite management and other key parties to a presentation of the study's findings.

Deciding on the ideal format for your communication requires thought. Even if you use a written format, you may find that supplementing a document with spoken communication will help you obtain the greatest impact.

You can use the worksheet "Focus Sheet" to keep your writing in touch with the writing principles.

WRITING FOR BUSINESS
Focus Sheet™
Answer these questions as the first step in any writing task.
Purpose
Why am I writing this?
What do I want the reader to do?
Audience
Who *exactly* is my reader? Do I have more than one?
What is the reader's role: Decision maker? Influencer? Implementer? Other?
What does the reader know about the subject?
How will the reader react to my main message: Receptive? Indifferent? Resistant?
What's in it for the reader? Why should the reader read this or agree with it?
How will the reader use this document?
Should anyone else receive this?

Bottom Line
If the reader were to forget everything else, what one main message must the reader remember?
So what? What is the impact of my bottom line?

Strategy
Should my message be a document? Or would a phone call be more effective?
Timing: Am I too early? Or too late to send it at all?
Distribution list: Trimmed to the minimum?
Is someone else communicating the same information? Should I check?

Select method(s) of transmission	
☐ E-mail	☐ Presentation
☐ Fax	☐ Videoconference
☐ Internal Mail	☐ Postal Delivery
☐ Intranet (Web sites or shared folders)	☐ Courier
☐ Internet	☐ Other:
☐ Meeting	

What You COULD Do

Deliver the Message

If you find yourself in Roger's position, you can't go wrong by using the first paragraph to state the key point or points you want to make, fleshing out the details in the paragraphs that follow. For example, you might begin as follows:

Here's the latest on the spring sales catalog: we plan to have advanced copies (25) in your hands by March 17. Customers will receive theirs the week beginning March 30. This catalog is a powerful selling tool, so be sure that you get your customers on our mailing list. We need their addresses no later than March 1!

Almost everyone will read the first paragraph, so put your main message there.

Scope Your Project

BEFORE YOU BEGIN writing any document, you should "scope" the project. Scoping means determining the breadth of your subject and deciding how deeply you will cover it. A good job of scoping will save you and your audience unnecessary time and work.

Broad versus limited scope

In scoping a project, you can look at your subject either broadly or narrowly. For example, a broad scope report on weaknesses in your company's marketing function might include the following:

- How marketing contributes to corporate goals
- Historical development of the company's marketing department
- Marketing's human resources
- Areas of specific performance problems
- Potential solutions

A limited-scope version of this topic would focus on only one or two areas:

- Two areas of underperformance: dealer support and promotions
- Suggested remedies

As a writer, you must determine how broad or limited the scope of your document should be, given your purpose and your audience. In the case of the marketing report, you might take a very broad approach if your purpose is to provide information to a task force assigned to reorient and strengthen the department. That audience would want to know as much as possible about the marketing department.

On the other hand, you'd probably use the limited-scope alternative if you were communicating to senior management about the task force's actual findings. In this case your audience would be most interested in the specifics about the problems you've identified and your recommended solutions. That's scoping!

Start-Up Strategies

FOR MANY PEOPLE, one of the hardest parts of writing is getting started. There are several strategies for overcoming that problem.

Questioning

One way to get started is to write down the questions your readers might have about your topic. This method helps you ensure that your document tells readers what they need to know. It also helps you anticipate readers' responses to your document.

For example, Gillian has to write a memo introducing a weekly interdepartmental meeting of employees involved with a new product launch. Trying to anticipate her readers' concerns, she produces the following questions:

- Why are we having these new meetings?
- What will be on the agenda?
- What do I need to prepare for the meetings?

By turning those questions into affirmative statements, Gillian can create the list of points she'll want to cover in her memo. For example, "For the first meeting, please come prepared with your unit's work plans."

If you use this method, consider your knowledge of the audience's interests and concerns. If you are not familiar with your audience, enlist someone with that familiarity to augment your list of anticipated questions.

The traditional outline

Another approach to getting starting is to use a traditional outline. This method seems to work best for people who can picture a logical document structure. It is especially useful for inexperienced writers or for people who must cover a complex subject.

A traditional outline uses letters and Roman and Arabic numerals to indicate levels of information.

1. Uppercase Roman numeral, period I.
2. Capital letter, period A.
3. Arabic numeral, period 1.
4. Lowercase letter, period a.
5. Arabic numeral in parentheses (1)
6. Lowercase letter in parentheses (a)
7. Lowercase Roman numeral in parentheses (i)

Three levels of headings (Roman numerals, capital letters, and Arabic numerals) are sufficient for most business documents.

Once you have an outline, ask yourself these questions:

- Have I listed all the topics and subtopics I need to cover?
- Are they arranged in a logical sequence?
- Is there a clear beginning, middle, and ending?

Once you are satisfied with the logic and flow of your outline, begin fleshing out each line to create your document.

The brainstorm outline

The brainstorm outline is a free-form technique for jotting down ideas as fast as they come into your mind. This free association helps boost your creativity. It is a particularly useful method when you're writing with a group, because it captures everyone's ideas at the beginning of the process. To create a brainstorm outline, follow these steps:

1. Draw a circle in the middle of a sheet of paper.
2. Write your purpose inside the circle. Your purpose is the reason you're writing the document. Keep it simple: start with the word *to* and include an action verb such as *persuade.*
3. As you think of ideas related to your topic, draw lines outward from the circle, like the spokes of a wheel, and write each idea on a line.
4. If an idea inspires related ideas, draw more lines off from that line and write your ideas on them.
5. If an idea comes to you that is entirely separate from the ideas you've written so far, draw a new line from the center circle.
6. Continue to generate ideas, drawing lines from the center circle and from other lines.

New product idea chart

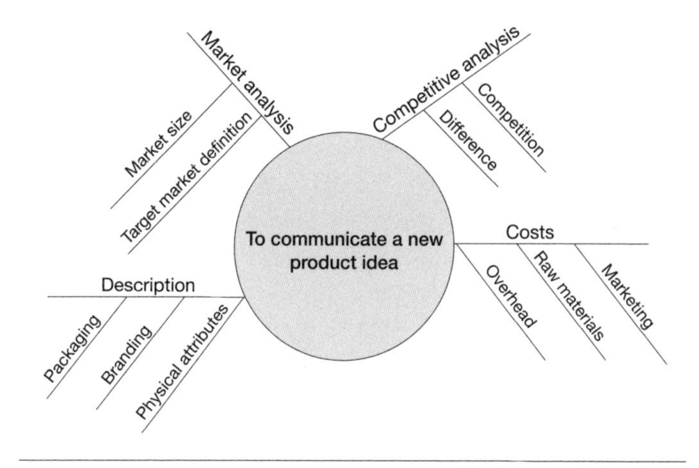

NOTE: Brainstorming is a technique used to generate ideas and solve problems. It can be used by individuals or groups. The term was coined in Alex Osborn's book, *Applied Imagination.*

Take care to define the main idea categories that come out of the center circle. Once you have them organized, those ideas will be the topics you'll want to cover.

Freewriting

Freewriting is often the best antidote for writer's block. Like the brainstorm outline, freewriting lets your imagination roam, thus facilitating the expression of great ideas, whether on paper or on screen. The most important rule to remember about freewriting is that *there are no rules.* To use the freewriting method, follow these steps:

1. Put pen to paper or fingers to keyboard, and let your mind wander.
2. Write down anything that comes into your mind, even if it has nothing to do with your writing topic.
3. Freewrite for at least ten minutes to get the ideas flowing.
4. When you get stuck, write that down, too. Don't stop.
5. Don't edit your work. If you're working at your computer, darkening the screen may help to keep you from editing prematurely.

When you've finished freewriting, read what you've set down, highlighting important points and ideas. Then organize those points into logical categories, just as you would in a traditional or brainstorming outline.

The "Abstract" Approach

One professional writer describes his approach to getting started.

> *When I have to write an article, a white paper, or extended report, I often begin by writing a one-page abstract. That abstract must describe in a nutshell the thesis of the article, mention the research or examples I'll use to support it, and state the consequences of my thesis for readers. I then refine that abstract to the point where everything hangs together and invites anyone to say, "This seems like something I should read." That abstract, in turn, acts as my compass, guiding more detailed development of the piece.*

Organize Material According to Purpose

WHAT YOU WRITE must be logically organized; otherwise, it won't accomplish the purpose you intended. By choosing the most appropriate organizing method, you can make your message clearer.

To start, consider the needs and preferences of your audience. Select an organization method by asking, and answering, questions such as these:

- What is my bottom line?
- Is my reader likely to be receptive or resistant?
- What might my reader want to know right away?

Order-of-importance method

Some writers use a "bottom line on top" (BLOT) approach for many internal documents. When you put the most critical information at the beginning, readers see your most important message quickly.

Chronological method

The chronological method of development describes a topic by listing events in the order in which they occurred. This approach is

Tips for Using the Order-of-Importance Method

- When writing for two or more readers, consider the probable reaction of the most important reader, usually the decision maker. Organize your document accordingly.
- For receptive readers, put your key message on top.
- For unreceptive or resistant readers, provide background before stating your key message. Use the document's beginning to convince readers that your recommendation is a good one.

useful for content such as the history of a product development project. When you use this method, remember these tips:

- Stick to major, consequential facts.
- Use visual design to highlight important information, such as your key message, which otherwise might get lost in this method of development.
- Avoid beginning each sentence with a date if there are more than five dates.

Process and procedure methods

The process and procedure methods are useful for instructions and for user manuals.

A **process** describes, in overview terms, who does what and what happens (or will happen) *in stages*. Because these stages occur independent of the reader, use the third person to describe them. For example, "An invoice goes first to the department that incurred the expense. Once approved, it moves to accounts payable."

A **procedure** provides action steps that the reader can actually *do*, in the order needed to accomplish the goal. Because a procedure is an arranged set of steps, present it in the same way you would a recipe or instructions for installing software. Use the imperative mood ("do this," "do that") when you describe the steps, and begin each step with an action verb. For example, "Date stamp the invoice" or, "Tear off the pink copy for your records."

When you use either of these methods, remember these tips:

- Put formal procedures in a table, and number each step.
- Present the stages or steps in the precise order in which they occur.

Spatial arrangement method

The spatial arrangement method is useful for trip reports, descriptions of machinery, and sales research. Think of it as a two- or three-dimensional map that helps readers understand your topic by taking them on a journey through it.

For example, to explain a company's sales territory plan you might first describe opportunities in Los Angeles, then new customers in Newark, and finally government prospects in Washington, D.C.

Tips for Using the Compare and Contrast Method

If you adopt the compare and contrast method, consider these tips:

- When you compare two subjects, mention the more familiar one first.
- Use graphs and charts to compare technical information.
- Don't mix advantages and disadvantages in the same section.
- Be coherent in your comparisons by using key phrases, such as "on one hand," "on the other hand," and "the latter."

When you use this method, remember these tips:

- Create a coherent and concrete order that's easy to follow, such as left to right, top to bottom, or exterior to interior.
- Use detail to create a visual image for your readers as you move them from space to space.
- Engage readers by varying sentences and substituting new phrases for overused ones.

Compare and contrast method

The compare and contrast method demonstrates how concepts are similar or different. It works well for feasibility studies, research results, and planning reports. It is especially effective when your aim is to evaluate the advantages and disadvantages of two alternatives.

For example, to communicate the pros and cons of two potential downtown office locations, you might adopt this sequence:

Advantages—site A and site B
Disadvantages—site A and site B

Specific-to-general or general-to-specific method

The specific-to-general or general-to-specific method is useful for work orders, training materials, and customer service letters. The key question to ask yourself is, "How much does my reader already know?" Once you've answered the question, begin your document with information familiar to the reader.

For example, suppose you're announcing a requirement that all department heads revise their monthly budgets. For the memo you will send to the accounting department, you might use the specific-to-general method. The accounting team initiated the requirement, so first restate the details of the revisions it requested; then address the effect of the revisions companywide. For all other departments, draft individual memos that move from a high-level description of the requirement to the specific changes each group must implement to provide a revised budget. Be sure to explain key terms that may be unfamiliar to readers.

When you use this method, remember these tips:

- Determine how much your readers already know about the subject.
- Begin your document with information familiar to readers.

- Move from specific to general for readers familiar with your topic.
- Move from general to specific for readers not familiar with your topic.
- Place the key message at the beginning whenever possible.

Analytical method

To use the analytical method, start by formulating a hypothesis and then rigorously test its truth through a questioning process. This method is useful for technical reports, annual reports, and financial analyses.

When you use this method, remember these tips:

- Be sure to include every aspect of your hypothesis to avoid being discredited—or worse, making a bad business decision.
- Analyze your data for similarities, differences, logical links, implications, and suggested actions.
- Simplify technical language for nontechnical readers, especially when you're writing a company report intended for the general public.

The worksheet "Document Organizing Guide" suggests which organizing approaches are most appropriate for various types of written communications.

WRITING FOR BUSINESS

Document Organizing Guide

Use this guide as a quick reference on organizing different sections of your document.

	Method of Organization						
Type of Document	**Order of importance**	**Chronology**	**Process**	**Organization in space**	**Compare/ contrast**	**Specific to general or vice versa**	**Analysis**
Accident Reports		X					
Analysis of Trends							X
Annual Reports	X						X
Audits	X						X
Customer Service Letters	X					X	
Demographic Studies				X			X
Descriptions			X	X			
Economic Forecasts	X						X
Feasibility Studies					X	X	X
Financial Analyses	X				X		X
Findings	X						
Growth Statistics		X					X
Handbooks			X	X			
Instructions			X	X			
Lab Reports	X	X	X		X		X
Minutes	X	X					
Problem-solving Memos	X						X
Procedures/ Processes		X	X	X			
Production Reports	X						
Progress Reports	X	X					
Proposals	X				X	X	
Research Results	X				X		
Sales Research Reports	X			X			
Technical Reports			X		X		X
Test Protocols		X					
Training		X	X		X	X	
Trip Reports	X	X		X			
Trouble Reports	X	X					X
User Manuals			X	X			
Work Orders		X			X		
Yearly Overviews	X	X			X		

Writing the First Draft

As you write your first draft, remember that it's more important to get it written than to get every detail right! The first draft can be rough in sentence structure, spelling, grammar, and punctuation. It's for your eyes only.

Getting it down in rough form has two benefits. First, it focuses your mind on the key ideas you intend to include. Second, because you will have only a small investment in a rough draft, you will feel more comfortable changing the order of your material—or discarding it altogether.

Begin where you feel most comfortable

There's no rule that says you must start *writing* at what will end up being the start of the piece. Keep your outline or plan in front of you, and use it to decide where you feel most comfortable starting. Most experienced writers save the introductory material until the end; it is often easier to compose an engaging opening paragraph after you know what your conclusions are.

Choose a headline, for example, and write a paragraph for it. When you've finished that, choose the next item you're comfortable writing, and so on. Stop periodically to compare your draft to your plan.

Write in categories

Writing an important letter can seem daunting when you don't have a method of breaking the task into manageable parts. Your writing is sure to improve if you look at it as a series of smaller tasks.

The following categories frequently appear in business letters, memos, and e-mail:

- Announcement of a change
- Background information
- Implementation plan
- Deadline
- Explanation of a process
- Results
- Conclusions
- Recommendations
- Observations
- Proposed actions
- Request for action
- Evaluation

A formal proposal includes these standard parts:

- Title page
- Table of contents
- Executive summary

- Introduction
- Statement of customer needs
- Proposed procedures (or technical plan)
- Benefits of the plan
- Impact of the plan
- Implementation plan
- Qualifications
- Cost analysis (or your investment)
- Statement of agreement
- Appendix

Tips for Writing a Proposal

- Before you begin, ask for a proposal planning session with the recipient in order to learn more about the company's needs.
- Make the customer the focus of your proposal. Tell your readers how your product or service will meet the customer's needs. Don't list all the features of your product or service, but match customer needs with your product's benefits and impact on the customer's business.
- Answer the "Why?" question.
- Be specific. The more concrete your information, the more real and workable your solution will appear.
- Design your proposal for visual impact.

Special considerations for a technical document

When writing a technical document for a nontechnical audience, spend extra time analyzing your readers. Ask yourself, "How much does the audience already understand about this topic?" Many writers use a two-column approach. Here's how it works. In one column, write the information for a technical reader. In the other, simplify and condense the information for a nontechnical reader.

Tips for Writing a Business Memo

- Cover only one topic per memo.
- Write a specific subject line.
- Use clear and specific headlines to highlight deadlines and action requests.
- Cluster related ideas into categories.
- Design your memo for visual impact.
- Use the active voice wherever possible.
- If you know your readers, your tone should be friendlier and less formal than in a business letter.

Structuring Paragraphs

PARAGRAPHS ARE THE essential building blocks of any document. They introduce topics and, in some cases, signal readers that another step in an argument has begun. In this way, paragraphs guide the reader. They also help you, the writer, keep your thinking clear and focused.

Limit the number of subjects in each paragraph

The control of subjects throughout your paragraphs is key to giving readers a sense of coherence and simplicity. Typically, a paragraph will have from three to a dozen sentences. Each of these sentences will have a subject.

Be careful to minimize the number of subjects used in one paragraph. Including more than three or four subjects in a paragraph will likely confuse readers.

Create smooth transitions

As you construct your paragraphs, think about how each one fits into the larger document. Smooth transitions between paragraphs, and between the sentences within paragraphs, can help readers see the link between ideas and the development of an argument.

Consider the following transitional sentence (in bold):

Proponents of expanding restaurant seating have failed to provide any estimates of construction, operating costs, and taxes. Without those estimates, any attempt to evaluate their proposal will be a waste of time.

Even if construction costs were reasonable and manageable for the operation, we would still be facing a high level of revenue uncertainty. *No one knows how a doubling of seating will affect annual revenues. Is it reasonable to assume that revenues will double, or is a 75 percent increase more likely?*

These sample paragraphs include two very different issues: the cost of expanding an existing restaurant, and how revenues might grow if such expansion were made. The transition statement provides readers with a smooth path between construction costs and revenue issues.

Between sentences, words or phrases can accomplish the same type of connection as the preceding sentence. Consider the following example of a transition (in bold):

Our inventory managers have kept a tight lid on finished goods stocks. ***Consequently,*** *working capital requirements have dropped by 8 percent.*

In this case, the term *consequently* establishes a causal relationship between the two sentences. Other useful transitions include *as a result, in addition, likewise, meanwhile, for example, finally, on the other hand, furthermore,* and *nevertheless.*

Tips for Writing a Business Letter

- Begin on a personal note.
- In the first sentence, grab your reader's attention with the key message.
- Keep sentence length to about twenty words or fewer.
- Use white space for easier scanning. Limit paragraphs to about five to six lines.
- Use the active rather than the passive voice.
- Adopt a positive tone. For example, use "your investment" instead of "fees" or "cost."
- Format your letter for visual impact.
- Toward the end, summarize your main points or suggest next steps for your readers.
- Don't mention enclosures in your opening sentence. If you send enclosures with your letter, mention them later in the body.
- Avoid an overly formal style.
- If appropriate, add a brief note of friendliness or a personal touch in your closing.

Editing for Content

I have rewritten—often several times—every word I have ever written. My pencils outlast their erasers.

—Vladimir Nabokov

YOUR GOAL IN WRITING a first draft is to set forth all the key ideas in a logical manner. Once you complete that draft, your next task is to edit its content. In the first editing pass, you finalize the structure, logic, and message of your document.

Put your message in focus

Writers often lose focus because they are unclear about what they want to say. If you are unclear in your own mind, how can you expect readers to understand? Another common mistake of writers is focusing on their own agendas and neglecting their readers' needs. To avoid these problems, review your first draft and ask yourself two questions:

- Is my key message clearly stated?
- Did I include all of the information my readers will need to understand what they need to do?

If the answer to either of these questions is no, review what you have already identified as your purpose, audience, and bottom line.

Edit your document to address your audience's requirements and to clearly state your key message.

Review for clarity

As you read the first draft, consider whether your purpose is easy to find and understand. Also review for precision and scope of content.

As you edit for clarity, ask yourself these questions:

- Is my information accurate?
- Is my information complete?
- Did I label requests for action and deadlines so that they will be obvious to the reader?
- Did I headline next steps?

Sequence your key message strategically

Another element to watch for is the location of your key message: the one thing you want readers to remember. In most cases, you should position this information at the beginning of the document. If the key message is buried, readers may skim right over it.

If you've determined that your reader will probably not be receptive to your ideas, position your key message strategically—where it will have the best chance of being read and considered. It may make more sense to build a context for your key message before introducing it.

Answer your readers' question: "Why?"

Your document not only should state your key message but also should explain why it is important. For example, if the key message is that you need more time to complete work on a project, don't just stop after you've explained your need. Answer the "Why?" question by including the following:

- What will happen if you don't get the extra time
- Whom your extension will affect
- How an extension will affect other projects you're working on
- How your readers will be affected

Don't skip the "Why?" question; it's your key to credibility. Make sure that your document explains exactly why your key message is important in terms that the reader will understand.

Be sure to include a clear statement of the impact of your key message in terms relevant to the audience. For example, instead of stating, "Option A is better than option B," write, "Option A is better than option B because option A will reduce annual operating costs by 30 percent."

Steps for Editing for Content

- Make sure that your message is audience focused.
- Review for clarity.
- Sequence your message strategically.
- Be sure you answer the question, "Why is this important?"

Editing for Style

To write simply is as difficult as to be good.

—W. Somerset Maugham

In this second stage of editing, your job is to make your writing sing. You do this by giving it visual appeal, giving it the right voice and tone, and making it accurate. Text with these qualities has an impact on readers.

Design for visual impact

By itself, clear and consistent writing is not enough to influence readers. They should be able find the key ideas at a glance, without searching through a lot of dense prose. When a document is easy to read and when key points jump out, it has visual impact.

Create a visual structure that entices your audience. Visual enhancements can make a message stand out from the hundreds that regularly bombard readers. The following are examples of visual enhancements:

- Headlines that highlight your most important points
- Sentences that are no more than twenty words long

- Short paragraphs and groups of sentences—five to six lines maximum
- Adequate white space
- Bold and italic typefaces that make important information stand out
- Bulleted or numbered lists
- Tables that organize complex information

One caution about visual enhancements: be careful when using e-mail or other electronic documents. Your reader may not have the programs to open your document in its intended format.

You can use the worksheet "Designing for Visual Impact Reference Guide" to help you design your documents for maximum effect.

Match your tone to your audience

The tone of your writing will influence readers' perception. For example, an informal tone may be appropriate for a colleague you know well, but a client or a supervisor might be put off by a message delivered in that tone.

The type of language you use will also impact your readers' understanding. Many writers use obscure or outdated language, believing it will make them sound more intelligent. Others choose longer words over shorter, simpler words for the same reason.

WRITING FOR BUSINESS

Designing for Visual Impact Reference Guide

Use this guide as a quick reminder of how to design your document for easy reading.

You Can Use . . .	To . . .
Headlines	• Introduce most paragraphs • Focus your reader on your major ideas
Sidelines	• Add extra emphasis • Aid in persuasion
Text Fonts	• Assure readability • Unify style
Short Paragraphs	• Avoid overwhelming your reader • Attract speed readers
Two Columns	• Convey two kinds of information simultaneously • Encourage faster reading
Bulleted Lists	• Replace lists within sentences
Numbered Lists	• Indicate sequence • List steps in a procedure • Provide easy reference to the list • Quantify items
White Space and Indentation	• Frame your ideas • Improve readability
Graphs, Charts, and Tables	• Present numbers, dollar amounts, and technical data
Color (use judiciously)	• Highlight information (limit to two colors) • Add aesthetic appeal
underlining, **bold typeface**, different fonts, ALL CAPITALS, *italics*, different type sizes	• Emphasize deadlines and action items

There's nothing wrong with wanting to sound intelligent. But clarity and simplicity—not overblown language—will better accomplish your objective. For example, consider this sentence:

> *We will convene an* advance planning *meeting,* brief in duration, *to* consolidate together *the work assigned to Nancy's committee before they forge onward.*

Here is a more straightforward version:

> *We will* meet briefly *to consolidate the work of Nancy's committee before the group continues.*

Check for conciseness

Just as your tone should be direct, the structure of your sentences and paragraphs should be concise.

As you review for conciseness, ask yourself these questions:

- Did I limit my paragraphs to six lines?
- Did I focus my paragraphs on one thought only?
- Did I limit my sentences to fifteen to twenty words?
- Did I eliminate as many unnecessary words as I could?

NOTE: "Omit unnecessary words." That's the advice William Strunk Jr. and E. B. White have given to generations of composition students in their classic *The Elements of Style*. Unnecessary words annoy readers, slow them down, and distract them from the key message. Be ruthless in eliminating unnecessary words.

Adopt the active voice

Voice indicates the relationship between a sentence's subject and its verb. When the subject acts, the sentence is in the active voice. When the subject is acted upon, you have the passive voice. The active voice results in a more forceful style. Consider the following sentences:

Active voice: We sent the customer a letter.
Passive voice: A letter to the customer was sent by us.

Here, the active voice has greater impact. Notice too that the active sentence uses fewer words to say the same thing than the passive sentence. It is also less formal and ponderous.

Passive sentences are not always bad; they are sometimes appropriate in impersonal reports and technical writing. But if you want to write with vigor and assertiveness, put most sentences in the active voice.

Edit for accuracy

An accurate document uses correct grammar, punctuation, and spelling. The grammar and spell-checking function of your word processing software can help here, but don't rely on it; it doesn't catch mistakes like using *their* in the place of *there* or *affect* for *effect*. One good way to catch errors is to ask a competent coworker to check your drafts of vital documents. Even the best writers benefit from objective editors.

Steps for Editing for Style

- Design for visual impact.
- Match your tone to your audience.
- Check for conciseness. State your message briefly but completely.
- Adopt the active voice.
- Edit for accuracy. Proofread carefully to make sure your grammar, punctuation, and spelling won't embarrass you.

The worksheet "'Be Your Own Editor' Checklist," shown on the next page, is useful when you edit your work.

WRITING FOR BUSINESS

"Be Your Own Editor" Checklist

The questions below reflect easy-to-overlook aspects of editing. Before releasing a document, verify for yourself that you have considered each item.

Content

Purpose:	☐ Stated clearly?	☐ Specific requests for action or information?
Information:	☐ Accurate and complete?	☐ Right amount of detail?

Sequence

Bottom Line:	☐ At the top?	☐ Strategically placed?
Organization:	☐ Ideas flow logically?	

Design

Format:	☐ Enough headlines, sidelines, and lists? ☐ White space to frame ideas?	☐ Deadlines and action items highlighted?
Presentation:	☐ Would a chart, table, or graph be more effective for certain information?	

Structure

Paragraphs:	☐ Begin with a topic sentence? ☐ Focused on one topic?	☐ Transitions within and between? ☐ Limited to 5 to 6 lines?
Sentences:	☐ Varied in structure and length?	☐ Streamlined to 15 to 20 words?

Tone/Style

Words:	☐ Simple, specific, and straightforward? ☐ Free of affectation and stuffy outdated language? ☐ Acronyms explained?	☐ Terminology familiar to readers? ☐ Headlines designed for impact?
Style:	☐ Personable, upbeat, and direct? ☐ Appropriate for the audience?	☐ Active voice? ☐ Positive approach?

Proofread

☐ Grammar, spelling, and punctuation accurate? ☐ Typographical errors corrected?	☐ Should someone else review this? ☐ If this is a repeat mailing, is new data highlighted?

Other *Enter your own editorial "trouble spots" to double-check and prevent.*

Drafting E-mail

IT'S SO EASY TO send e-mail that sometimes it doesn't seem like writing at all. But you should give e-mail correspondence the same kind of attention you give business letters, memos, and reports. Here we'll consider some typical problems and things you can do to make your e-mail more effective.

Common problems

E-mail has become the dominant method of communication in many companies because it's fast, easy, and inexpensive. Unfortunately, the speed and ease of e-mail have also created some problems for business writers and their companies:

- Employees send and receive time-wasting, unnecessary messages.
- Many e-mails are poorly and hastily written.
- Writers sometimes dash off messages that are emotional or inappropriate in a business setting.
- Messages are occasionally misdirected or forwarded to unintended recipients, sometimes with negative consequences.
- Some e-mails are read so quickly that recipients miss important details.

E-mail senders can avoid these problems by using common-sense writing principles.

Start with the subject line

The subject line is the headline for your message, the lure that gets your reader interested and involved. Take the time to write a subject line that does four things:

- Contains the key message ("Sales meeting rescheduled to 3 p.m. Friday")
- Includes your desired action or response ("Comments needed by 4 p.m. today")
- Is specific but not too long ("Lunch tomorrow?")
- Allows your reader to file and retrieve your message easily ("John's global enterprise report")

If your subject line is too general or vague, the reader may skip your message. If the subject line is blank, the reader may delete it. Remember: busy people often receive fifty to one hundred e-mail messages per day. To ensure that yours is opened and read, you must make it stand out.

Only one topic per e-mail

Treat each e-mail as a coherent information packet—to ask a question, communicate your opinion, report news, and so on. To

What Would YOU Do?

Blindspots

CINDY'S COWORKERS ARE usually supportive, but lately they aren't following through on her requests. She doesn't understand why. Two weeks ago, when she e-mailed the conference summary to the team, she included a note scheduling a Friday morning team meeting. When Friday arrived, however, only two people showed up. A week later, Cindy e-mailed everyone again, this time about monthly reports. In her message she included a note about executives visiting the staff meetings. The team members acted surprised when the vice president of corporate sales attended the next meeting. Are Cindy's teammates ignoring her? Or is she simply not getting through to them? What would you do?

---

be coherent, your e-mail should contain only one message. This approach has two advantages:

- Recipients can digest and respond to a single message more easily.
- The recipient can forward the message without dragging along other messages that may be highly inappropriate for the audience.

Make the purpose of the message clear

Convey your purpose to the reader immediately—in the subject line *and* at the start of the message. Let your reader know whether it's a call to action, a request for information, a sharing of information, or a recommendation.

Be concise and use attachments

Long e-mail messages require lots of annoying on-screen scrolling by the recipient. So keep your messages short. When you have a lengthy message, send it as an attachment instead of as e-mail text. Use the e-mail message to tell the reader what the attachment is and what the reader should do with it. Here's an example:

> *Hello, Charlene:*
> *My first draft of the customer survey report is attached.*
> *Please review and return it with your comment by Thursday.*
> *Thanks, Howard*

Remember your audience

When writing to your peers and friends, you can be as informal as you want. When writing to a superior or client, make your e-mail look like a brief professional memo. Adapt your tone and language to the reader.

Keep formatting simple

In the e-mail environment, you can't control how a message will appear on the recipient's screen, so don't expect fancy formatting to be maintained in the transfer. For headlines or emphasis, capitalize all letters. (However, don't send your entire message in all caps. That's considered shouting.) Use white space to help the reader grasp the message quickly; it's difficult to read a lot of text bunched together.

Review your company's e-mail policy

Despite its great convenience for businesses, e-mail may make a company vulnerable to lawsuits for harassment and libel. As a result, many companies have a policy that clearly outlines how e-mail should be used at work. Find out whether your company has such a policy.

Know when *not* to send an e-mail

E-mail may be the preferred form of communication in many organizations, but it's not always the most effective or appropriate method. In addition to following your company's e-mail policies, consider these suggestions:

- Avoid sending private messages via e-mail. For personal or confidential exchanges, call or meet the person.
- Arrange a face-to-face meeting when e-mail messages don't seem to be working effectively. If you keep sending mes-

sages back and forth without reaching a resolution—whether over a period of hours or a number of weeks—then pick up the telephone and make an appointment to meet. A general guideline is to limit your e-mail exchanges to no more than four.

- Delete mass mailings; don't forward them.

Be particularly careful when you're expressing emotion in e-mail. Humor can be misunderstood, criticism may be misinterpreted, and angry feelings can be further inflamed. If you aren't sure whether your intention will be understood, don't send the message. A face-to-face meeting or phone call may be a better choice.

Tips for Writing an E-mail Message

- Put the key message in your subject line to ensure that your reader doesn't delete your message.
- Keep your message short. Try to put all the pertinent information on the first screen.
- Cover only one topic per e-mail.
- Edit and spell-check your message before sending it.
- Never send e-mail when you're angry. A good test is to ask yourself whether you would make your statement to the person's face. If not, don't send the message electronically.
- When forwarding a message, check the original subject line. Will the new reader understand the topic? If not, revise as needed.

- Include a closing. For external readers, use something simple such as "Sincerely" or "Regards." For internal messages, follow your organization's guidelines.
- Type the recipient's address just before you click Send. This reduces the chance that you'll send an unfinished message or a message to the wrong person.
- Send e-mails only to people who need to receive them.

What You COULD Do.

Focus Your Message

Cindy may not be connecting with her teammates because she's trying to convey too much information in her e-mails. As a rule, each message should cover only one topic. If the e-mail covers multiple topics and is lengthy, readers may get lost and not read the entire e-mail. Cindy should also clarify the purpose of the message, both in the subject line and at the beginning of the message. If she wants people to attend a meeting, she should call that to their attention immediately. Cindy should also make her e-mails concise. Brevity is usually in everybody's best interest.

Tips and Tools

Tools for Business Writing

WRITING FOR BUSINESS

Focus Sheet™

Answer these questions as the first step in any writing task.

Purpose

Why am I writing this?

What do I want the reader to do?

Audience

Who *exactly* is my reader? Do I have more than one?

What is the reader's role: Decision maker? Influencer? Implementer? Other?

What does the reader know about the subject?

How will the reader react to my main message: Receptive? Indifferent? Resistant?

What's in it for the reader? Why should the reader read this or agree with it?

How will the reader use this document?

Should anyone else receive this?

Bottom Line
If the reader were to forget everything else, what one main message must the reader remember?
So what? What is the impact of my bottom line?

Strategy
Should my message be a document? Or would a phone call be more effective?
Timing: Am I too early? Or too late to send it at all?
Distribution list: Trimmed to the minimum?
Is someone else communicating the same information? Should I check?

Select method(s) of transmission	
☐ E-mail	☐ Presentation
☐ Fax	☐ Videoconference
☐ Internal Mail	☐ Postal Delivery
☐ Intranet (Web sites or shared folders)	☐ Courier
☐ Internet	☐ Other:
☐ Meeting	

Document Organizing Guide

Use this guide as a quick reference on organizing different sections of your document.

	Method of Organization						
Type of Document	**Order of importance**	**Chronology**	**Process**	**Organization in space**	**Compare/ contrast**	**Specific to general or vice versa**	**Analysis**
Accident Reports		X					
Analysis of Trends							X
Annual Reports	X						X
Audits	X						X
Customer Service Letters	X					X	
Demographic Studies				X			X
Descriptions			X	X			
Economic Forecasts	X						X
Feasibility Studies					X	X	X
Financial Analyses	X				X		X
Findings	X						
Growth Statistics		X					X
Handbooks			X	X			
Instructions			X	X			
Lab Reports	X	X	X		X		X
Minutes	X	X					
Problem-solving Memos	X						X
Procedures/ Processes		X	X	X			
Production Reports	X						
Progress Reports	X	X					
Proposals	X				X	X	
Research Results	X				X		
Sales Research Reports	X			X			
Technical Reports			X		X		X
Test Protocols		X					
Training		X	X		X	X	
Trip Reports	X	X		X			
Trouble Reports	X	X					X
User Manuals			X	X			
Work Orders		X			X		
Yearly Overviews	X	X			X		

WRITING FOR BUSINESS

Designing for Visual Impact Reference Guide

Use this guide as a quick reminder of how to design your document for easy reading.

You Can Use . . .	To . . .
Headlines	• Introduce most paragraphs • Focus your reader on your major ideas
Sidelines	• Add extra emphasis • Aid in persuasion
Text Fonts	• Assure readability • Unify style
Short Paragraphs	• Avoid overwhelming your reader • Attract speed readers
Two Columns	• Convey two kinds of information simultaneously • Encourage faster reading
Bulleted Lists	• Replace lists within sentences
Numbered Lists	• Indicate sequence • List steps in a procedure • Provide easy reference to the list • Quantify items
White Space and Indentation	• Frame your ideas • Improve readability
Graphs, Charts, and Tables	• Present numbers, dollar amounts, and technical data
Color (use judiciously)	• Highlight information (limit to two colors) • Add aesthetic appeal
underlining, **bold typeface**, different fonts, ALL CAPITALS, *italics*, different type sizes	• Emphasize deadlines and action items

WRITING FOR BUSINESS

"Be Your Own Editor" Checklist

The questions below reflect easy-to-overlook aspects of editing. Before releasing a document, verify for yourself that you have considered each item.

Content

Purpose: ☐ Stated clearly? ☐ Specific requests for action or information?

Information: ☐ Accurate and complete? ☐ Right amount of detail?

Sequence

Bottom Line: ☐ At the top? ☐ Strategically placed?

Organization: ☐ Ideas flow logically?

Design

Format: ☐ Enough headlines, sidelines, and lists? ☐ White space to frame ideas? ☐ Deadlines and action items highlighted?

Presentation: ☐ Would a chart, table, or graph be more effective for certain information?

Structure

Paragraphs: ☐ Begin with a topic sentence? ☐ Focused on one topic? ☐ Transitions within and between? ☐ Limited to 5 to 6 lines?

Sentences: ☐ Varied in structure and length? ☐ Streamlined to 15 to 20 words?

Tone/Style

Words: ☐ Simple, specific, and straightforward? ☐ Free of affectation and stuffy outdated language? ☐ Acronyms explained? ☐ Terminology familiar to readers? ☐ Headlines designed for impact?

Style: ☐ Personable, upbeat, and direct? ☐ Appropriate for the audience? ☐ Active voice? ☐ Positive approach?

Proofread

☐ Grammar, spelling, and punctuation accurate?
☐ Typographical errors corrected?
☐ Should someone else review this?
☐ If this is a repeat mailing, is new data highlighted?

Other *Enter your own editorial "trouble spots" to double-check and prevent.*

Test Yourself

Following are ten multiple-choice questions to help you see what you've learned and to identify areas that you may want to explore further. Answers to the questions follow.

1. Which of the following topics would be best served by a broadly scoped report?

a. Communicating the findings of a task force on pricing to your company's top management.

b. Informing a newly formed task force about pricing issues facing your company.

c. Convincing a sales team of the need to create a pricing task force at your company.

2. What is meant by "reader-centered writing"?

a. "Reader-centered writing" means writing to the reader as if you were speaking face-to-face.

b. "Reader-centered writing" means considering a reader's needs at every step of the writing process.

c. "Reader-centered writing" means repeating the purpose for writing throughout a document to reinforce the rationale in readers' minds.

3. Which of the following is a recommended strategy for writing a first draft?

a. Start at the beginning of the document, and systematically work your way through your outline.

b. Break your document into categories, and work through each one at your own pace.

c. Break your document into sections, and perfect each section before starting to work on the next one.

4. Which of the following statements illustrates a common style error made by many writers?

a. "This customer-focused strategy can give us a big lead on the competition."

b. "Developing a stand-alone distribution channel rather than using our existing shipping center could save us up to 30% on our annual costs."

c. "It is essential that you keep in mind that this solution was designed and developed by the chief engineer."

5. Lengthy sentences can be cumbersome or cause your reader to lose the key message. What is a good guideline for sentence length?

a. About twenty words.

b. About twenty-five to thirty words.

c. Fifteen words or fewer.

6. Which of the following is not a recommended start-up strategy?

a. Write a brainstorm outline.

b. Craft an excellent first sentence.

c. Write a traditional outline.

7. Because e-mail is widespread and easy to use, it's tempting to fall into the trap of exchanging e-mails endlessly with a team member to resolve an issue instead of making the effort to communicate in person. At what point should you stop e-mailing and start communicating face-to-face, or at least by phone?

a. In general, no more than four exchanges.

b. After two exchanges.

c. If the issue is unresolved in three business days.

8. You are preparing to write a paragraph of average length. How many subjects should you include?

a. Only one.

b. More than four.

c. Between two and four.

9. You have been asked to write a memo describing the flow of information during the review cycle of an upcoming project. Which organizational method would better suit your purpose: procedure or process?

a. Process, describing who does what and what happens.

b. Procedure, using a sequenced set of steps beginning with action verbs, similar to a recipe.

c. Either will accomplish the objective.

10. Jane is planning a memo that will ask her readers to stay late for an after-work meeting next week. She knows that most of the people who will receive this memo will be resistant to her request. Where should she put the key message?

a. Right at the beginning to make her point.

b. Somewhere in the middle, using the beginning of the document to set the context of her request.

c. In the subject line only; she should use the content of the memo to persuade and convince the readers.

Answers to test questions

1, b. Informing a newly formed task force about pricing issues facing your company.

In this case, your purpose is to get the readers up to speed on the issues. This audience would want to know as much as possible about the subject, because the task force will be reviewing the issue in detail. As a writer, you must determine how broad or limited the scope of your document should be, given your purpose and your audience; in this case, a broad scope would provide the readers with the background they need.

2, b. "Reader-centered writing" means considering a reader's needs at every step of the writing process.

In other words, it means writing from the readers' points of view. Imagining that you are the various readers helps you anticipate the kinds of questions they might have. Thinking from their perspective also helps you avoid the chief complaint of business readers: not knowing what the writer wants from them.

3, b. Break your document into categories, and work through each one at your own pace.

The task of writing an important document can seem daunting when you don't have a method for breaking it down into manageable parts. Your writing will improve when you begin to look at writing as a series of smaller tasks, and work through each one at your own pace.

4, c. "It is essential that you keep in mind that this solution was designed and developed by the chief engineer."

This sentence uses the passive voice as well as unneeded words. It would have more impact if it simply read, "Please note that the chief engineer designed and developed this solution."

5, a. About twenty words.

It's a good idea to limit sentences to about twenty words, and paragraphs to about six lines. That number may seem low, but it is not difficult to break one sentence into two and add white space every five to six lines.

6, b. Craft an excellent first sentence.

Spending time crafting an excellent first sentence is not a recommended strategy. It makes more sense to use a strategy that helps you develop a structure for the document. The four recommended strategies are (1) writing a traditional outline, (2) writing a brainstorm outline, (3) imagining yourself in the reader's shoes and answering the questions you would ask, and (4) freewriting.

7, a. In general, no more than four exchanges.

If you find you've been e-mailing back and forth with a coworker or team member several times, it could be a clue that you're avoiding a resolution or a decision. Discuss the issue in person or on the phone.

8, c. Between two and four.

Effective writers include between two and four subjects in an average-length paragraph. Trying to cover more than four subjects will likely confuse your reader.

9, a. Process, describing who does what and what happens.

To find the clue that process is the better choice, examine the requested task. The request was to describe a flow of information rather than explain how to accomplish a job. A procedure is appropriate when you need to write a sequenced set of steps to explain how to accomplish a specific task.

10, b. Somewhere in the middle, using the beginning of the document to set the context of her request.

When you know that readers may be resistant, the recommended choice is to first build a context for the needed action. In this case, Jane should use the beginning of the memo to describe the situation. After she has convinced her readers of the importance of having a meeting the following week, and of the scheduling issues that make a workday meeting impossible, she should ask her participants to attend.

To Learn More

Articles

Clayton, John. "Five Quick Ways to Trim Your Writing." *Harvard Management Communication Letter,* April 2003.

At the eleventh hour, you must make a critical report 30 percent leaner. How can you do it quickly? These five tips will help you cut length without cutting meaning.

Donahue, Kristen B. "Misused Words and Other Writing Gaffes: A Manager's Primer." *Harvard Management Communication Letter,* November 2001.

Managers are valued for their leadership, management skills, and vision, not for their adherence to the rules of grammar and punctuation. And yet the ability to communicate via the written word is crucial. Mistakes in grammar, clunky phrasing, and carelessness can muddle your message and undermine your credibility. Learning the most common writing mistakes, and how you can avoid them, will improve your writing and communications skills.

Harvard Business School Publishing. "The Ten Commandments of Writing." *Harvard Management Communication Letter*, November 2000.

Write powerful, exciting prose with these ten tried-and-true rules.

Henning, Kathy. "Brevity Isn't Enough—You Need to Write Tight." *Harvard Management Communication Letter*, February 2003.

Eliminating words when you write doesn't guarantee clarity. What you should be doing is cutting wordiness. If you don't understand the difference, read this expert advice on writing tight. You need clarity, accuracy, relevance, sincerity, concision, transparency, and consistency to make your writing tighter—and better.

Kinni, Theodore. "Ayn Rand on Writing." *Harvard Management Communication Letter*, January 2003.

Although Ayn Rand is best known for her two popular novels on ideas, she devoted much of her later life to writing nonfiction. She believed that the most important elements of effective nonfiction writing were "clarity, clarity, and clarity." In this insightful article, read five tips for writing as clearly and as powerfully as Rand herself.

Morgan, Nick. "Writing Well When Time Is Tight." *Harvard Management Communication Letter*, May 2002.

Putting together a clear, compelling presentation of your ideas is easier than it might seem, even if you're no wordsmith and are facing a deadline. This article explains how basic organizational principles can help you get your ideas on paper in a way that's organized and persuasive.

Books

Dumaine, Deborah. *Vest-Pocket Guide to Business Writing.* Englewood Cliffs, NJ: Prentice-Hall, 1997.

This portable A-to-Z guide is packed with real-life examples of effective business writing. Entries cover everything from formatting documents to writing winning sales proposals. Readers benefit from Dumaine's twenty-year career of coaching businesspeople globally.

Harvard Business School Publishing. *The Manager's Guide to Effective Business Writing. Harvard Management Communication Letter Collection.* Boston: Harvard Business School Publishing, 2000.

This comprehensive collection from *Harvard Management Communication Letter* offers eight articles on effective business writing.

Houp, Kenneth W., Thomas E. Pearsall, Elizabeth Tebeaux, and Sam Dragga. *Reporting Technical Information.* 10th ed. New York: Oxford University Press, 2002.

Topics include business correspondence, job hunting, report writing, instructions, proposals, progress reports, and oral presentations. The authors practice what they preach; their technical information is presented in an easy-to-read format.

University of Chicago Press Staff. *The Chicago Manual of Style: The Essential Guide for Writers, Editors, and Publishers.* 15th ed. Chicago: University of Chicago Press, 2003.

This classic reference is an invaluable tool for all writers. It offers comprehensive, consistent guidelines, as well as many examples of correct grammar and usage.

Sources for Business Writing

Buzan, Tony, with Barry Buzan. *The Mind Map: How to Use Radiant Thinking to Maximize Your Brain's Untapped Potential.* Paris: Plume, 1996.

Dumaine, Deborah. *Vest-Pocket Guide to Business Writing.* Englewood Cliffs, NJ: Prentice-Hall, 1997.

Dumaine, Deborah. *Write to the Top: Writing for Corporate Success.* New York: Random House, 1989.

Harvard Business School Publishing. *Business Communication.* Boston: Harvard Business School Press, 2004.

Notes

How to Order

Harvard Business School Press publications are available worldwide from your local bookseller or online retailer.

You can also call:
1-800-668-6780

Our product consultants are available to help you 8:00 a.m.–6:00 p.m., Monday–Friday, Eastern Time. Outside the U.S. and Canada, call: 617-783-7450.

Please call about special discounts for quantities greater than ten.

You can order online at:
www.HBSPress.org